Worship Guitar In Six Weeks

A Complete Beginner's Guide to Learning Rhythm Guitar for Christian Worship Music

MICAH BROOKS

WORSHIPHEART

PUBLISHING | EST. 1985

Copyright Information

Published by WorshipHeart Publishing

© 2016 Micah Brooks Kennedy | WorshipHeart Publishing

For written permission contact WorshipHeart Publishing at: www.worshippublishing.com or email info@worshippublishing.com

Photos by Micah Brooks Kennedy and Rochelle Marie Kennedy

Drawings by Amy Roberts

ISBN #: 978-0-9971940-1-2

Resources

Find out about the other books in this series and sign up for the Micah Brooks "Stay Connected" mailing list.

This is book one in the Micah Brooks Guitar Authority Series books. This first book, *Worship Guitar In Six Weeks,* is a six week course designed to bring a guitar player from knowing little about guitar onto the stage in six weeks. The second book is *42 Guitar Chords Everyone Should Know. Guitar Secrets Revealed* is the third book and is intended to be for intermediate to experienced guitar players.

Find out about the Micah Brooks Guitar Authority Series books and more at:

www.micahbrooks.com

Email Micah

Email Micah Brooks at micah@micahbrooks.com. I want to know who you are. I have a heart to meet people. It is my privilege to respond to my emails personally. Please feel free to connect with me. I will glad to answer questions or set up a Skype call as you need.

Join the Micah Brooks "Stay Connected" mailing list

Subscribe to the Micah Brooks Ministry "Stay Connected" mailing list and stay current with my latest book releases. My email list is always free and intended to deliver high value content to your inbox. I do not sell your email address to anyone else. I simply want to be able to stay connected with you. Click here to join my mailing list.

www.micahbrooks.com/join

Reviews on Amazon

Reviews are the lifeblood of authors. If you are willing to leave feedback, I would be humbled and grateful. Please do so at:

www.amazon.com

Skype Lessons

I would be glad to consider giving you online guitar lessons. If you would like to apply for lessons with Micah Brooks via Skype visit my website to find out more. I cannot accept every student, but I would be happy to hear your story and see what you would like to accomplish. Visit micahbrooks.com.

Join The Christian Guitar Community Facebook Group

All readers of this book are welcome to join The Christian Guitar Community Facebook group. Meet guitar players from around the world. You may post your insights about learning guitar. You are welcome to ask questions and comment on other posts. The group is designed to be a community. We ask everyone in the group to interact, which makes the content fun and engaging.

www.facebook.com/groups/thechristianguitarcommunity

Visit **micahbrooks.com** for more about Micah Brooks including books, CDs, mp3s, online store, speaking and performing dates.

Dedication

A very special thank you to my wife Rochelle and my children Liam, Aisley and Jovie. Without you this would not have been possible. To you my deepest love and affection.

Table Of Contents

- - - - -

Introduction

Welcome to Worship Guitar In Six Weeks! I am excited that you've decided to learn to play guitar. It's thrilling to tell you that in six weeks you will certainly be able to. There is great need for worship guitarists! Having the skill to play songs for the Lord is an excellent pursuit and one I'm certain the Lord accepts as noble. After working through this material, you should be able to perform for campfire worship retreats, small group settings, Sunday school, Sunday morning worship services and many other worship experiences. Imagine someone saying: "I wish someone could play a few worship songs for us tonight." Now that's you! I promise, if you will devote 10 minutes each day for six weeks you will master these thirteen chords and techniques. You will be able to play at least 75% of the worship songs you know and love.

Before we dive in, I always begin any of my guitar lessons with prayer. The reason is simple but important. With all my heart I believe that God created music. He created music for the purpose of allowing us to express ourselves in worship before Him. To allow us to be creative before Him. David demonstrated this hundreds of times in the Old Testament. Please let me pray over you:

"Lord Jesus, I thank You for this precious guitarist and their desire to honor You through guitar and worship music. I pray that as they are diligent in learning this craft, You would add to their learning. May You ignite in them a passion for Your name and a desire to please You through music. Please work in them as they use their new ability to glorify You and extend Your kingdom. In Jesus' name, amen."

- - - - -

WEEK ONE (1)

Each week we will begin our lesson with a prayer to be spoken aloud and for your benefit. Praying daily before you begin is an excellent way to invite the Lord into your learning. In doing so, he may help you learn at a greater pace. Let's begin week one.

Daily Prayer For WEEK ONE

"Heavenly Father, thank you for this day that you have made. I rejoice and am glad in it! Please go before me as I learn about guitar as a craft. May I choose the perfect instrument to suit my new abilities. Help me to understand and remember each of the parts of my guitar and be able to maintain this instrument well. Holy Spirit, remind me of good posture each time I perform. May I understand new concepts. I pray that you would help my hands to adjust well to playing each chord I learn. In Jesus' name, amen."

WHAT TO EXPECT WEEK ONE

By the end of week one you should know each of the many parts of your guitar by name. You should understand guitar tuning and how to properly hold your instrument. Plus, you will know your first chord: "G". Week one has the most information to read, but if you stay focused you'll have laid a guitar foundation to build upon. Each week trades less and less information for more and more application. This is intentional. Feel free to break up some of the information sections into the days of your first few weeks. The important part is that you comprehend the information, not that you race to get it all in one sitting.

Let's Begin

As you study this material, I believe you will notice that music is both artistic and mathematical. It utilizes both sides of the brain. God designed it to have a sense of free form and order all in one. Music is built upon 12 notes that repeat throughout the entire universe. 8 of these notes create an octave, and only 5 or sometimes 6 of these are used in popular music. So, how can there be so many songs if only 5 notes were used to create them? That is the simple, yet complex nature of God's design.

I believe that talent is something God-given. Something that you discover, while skill is something that you have to develop. While God instills talent, you shape your skill through trial and error. This is called learning. Even the light bulb took over a thousand tries before Edison landed on his final invention.

As we begin, please remember that anything worth doing takes time, effort and perseverance. Remember this as your fingers become sore or if you cannot master a chord on the first try. By the end of week one you will have accomplished something of value. IMPORTANT: You can play guitar, it will just take time.

Parts Of The Guitar

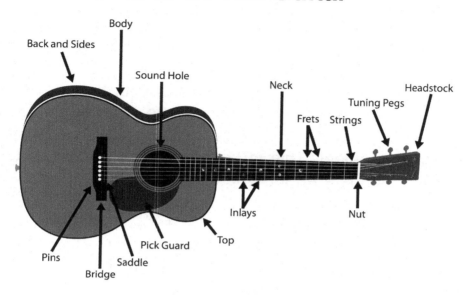

Parts Of The Guitar

Every musical instrument is made of several parts, similar to how the car is the sum of its parts. Each piece works in harmony with the others to create sympathetic vibration in the atmosphere. In other words sound. Most guitars are made of porous, malleable wood that is glued together. While your guitar may have some plastic parts on it, most likely the important parts are made of wood.

Let's talk about the guitar as a whole and then we'll dive in to the three main sections a little deeper.

Your guitar's parts are much like yours. There is a head, neck and body. While there are not any legs or arms for standard guitars being sold by the publishing date of this book, strange guitars are being produced all the time. So there may be guitars with hands and feet soon enough.

Headstock

The top of your guitar is called the headstock. Much like your own head, this is where it all comes together. You'll usually find six tuning pegs in two rows of three. If all your tuners are on the same side that's okay too. That would be another configuration that guitars come in. Tuning pegs, or tuners, are usually made of strong stainless steel. This is because there is a lot of tension when guitar strings are taut. The tuning pegs need to be able to hold all of the tension to keep the guitar in tune. If your tuners aren't keeping the strings in tune then it's time to head to the music shop. You need your instrument fixed. You'll be frustrated until you do. Being constantly out of tune is no fun.

The last part of the headstock is the nut. The nut is the transitioning piece that joins the head to the neck. It is one of two pieces with intentionally laid out grooves. The nut is also one of the two places where the guitar strings actually touch the guitar. This piece is usually made from strong plastic or even animal bone. The nut must remain securely fastened to the bottom of the headstock in order to keep the strings at the proper angle for pressing down. If the nut on your guitar is coming off or separated from your headstock, then back to the guitar store you go. This needs to be a solid and strong part of your guitar.

Neck

The neck is the part of the guitar with all the frets. Frets are thin strips of metal, usually stainless steel, that are slightly raised from the playable area of the neck. Your guitar will normally have 16-22 frets. You will typically use only 12 of those frets, so don't trade your guitar in if you only have 14 frets. Sometimes there are pieces of plastic or even pearl that have been built into your fretboard called inlays. These are typically spaced on the 3rd, 5th, 7th, 9th, 12th and 15th frets. They are there as guides to remind you at quick glance which fret you are on. Often there are little dots on the top side of the binding of the neck. You may use these as finger positioning guides as well. Again, don't worry if you only have a few of these dots or even none at all.

Some professional guitarists will tell you that the wood used for the fretboard of the neck is extremely important. While they would be correct when you are considering a $5,000 instrument, I don't think it's as important on an entry level or even an intermediate guitar. I think what is most important is that you like the size and feel of the neck and fretboard. Some necks are U-shaped and typically feel smaller. Others are C-shaped and take a larger hand to get around. There is no right or wrong on this. Choosing a neck is based upon your preference.

Body

The body is the largest part of the guitar. This is where most of the wood is pieced together. There are several parts to the body. The biggest are the back and sides and then the top. The back and sides are usually made of a harder wood, like mahogany. The top on the other hand is usually a much more porous wood, like spruce or rosewood. There are very specific reasons for this. Guitars are made for vibration. When you hold a guitar, most of the time you are touching the back and sides with your leg or forearm. That contact is deadening most of the vibrations, so not much of your guitar's sound vibrates from the back and sides. The top (also known as the front of the guitar) is not typically being touched by anything. This allows for the most vibration. Since that is the case, usually the most expensive piece of wood on your guitar is the top. I recommend that you use a guitar with a good top. You can usually tell by how good a guitar is by how much vibration happens when you strum the strings. If there isn't much sustaining of sound then the top is not very good. If it holds the sound for 7 seconds or more then you may have found a nice top, which makes for a nicer instrument.

The bridge is a piece that is glued to the top and is the only other place that the strings constantly touch the guitar. Located on the bridge is the saddle, which has six little string pins that look a bit like teeth when you pull them out. Your saddle and bridge should be fully fastened to the top of the guitar, like the nut on the headstock. If yours is pulling away from the top then you're headed once more to the store. I hope they aren't starting to get to know you there because of needing to fix your broken guitar…

The last parts of the body that you will notice are the parts that are not as easily visible. The sound hole is the void in the middle of the wood where your strings cross the body on their way to the saddle. This lets sound into the body of the guitar and allows the top to resonate. You may see guitars that have the sound hole in odd places. Those guitars are made with such precision that sound vibrates without needing the sound hole to be directly over the strings. They are usually priced on the higher end of the guitar pricing spectrum. Alongside the sound hole is a protective guard, called the pick guard. This protects the wood on the top from being scraped by finger nails and guitar picks.

Deep inside the sound hole are braces. They look like they've been placed there randomly, but they are actually engineered to be in that particular pattern. The theory is that sound will bounce around inside the guitar at certain intervals. The braces are spaced to either enhance or inhibit certain frequencies. The result is an even and louder tone building within the instrument.

There are a few optional parts your guitar may or may not have. One is either a set of two or simply one strap pin. These allow you to connect a guitar strap to your guitar for playing standing up. The other optional part of your guitar that you may or may not have is a cutaway. This is literally a part of the guitar that has been cut away from the body. The sole purpose of this is to let you reach those upper 14-21 frets with your fretting hand. The cutaway leaves less room for sound to vibrate therefore it may lesson some of the instruments lower end sound and accentuate the higher end.

Holding Your Guitar (Posture)

Learning how to hold your guitar properly is extremely important. Holding your guitar in the correct manner will help you reach all your chords with ease and cut down on finger and hand pain. Those who are prone to carpal tunnel should be careful to always keep good guitar posture.

While you may want to try variations of this technique, this will certainly get you started. Begin by being seated. Place the body of the guitar, where it bends in the middle, directly onto your right thigh. Remember to reverse these positions for left handed players. Let the upper body rest on your rib cage. Now the guitar should have a solid foundation. Always do your best to keep your back straight and a long back of neck with your head angled slightly downward. While this won't improve your guitar playing posture necessarily, it is widely accepted as the best singing posture. This posture may help you down the road if you want to sing and play at the same time.

Next, let your left hand hold the top of the neck. You may grip around the neck to offer support. Lastly, let your right arm hang over the sound hole. Your right elbow should be bent just barely touching the top of the body of your guitar. You should now be in an excellent seated guitar playing posture.

If you want to stand and play, which is a little more difficult, make sure that the strap you own has been correctly attached. It needs to bear the weight of your guitar by itself. You don't want your guitar to fall to the ground and break into a million pieces. This

19

isn't a rock show. When you stand and play, you want to keep the same posture with your right and left hands as you did while sitting. The difference is that the guitar will not rest on your leg any longer but will be supported by your right shoulder and will rest on the front of your right hip.

Whether sitting or standing, you will want your right hand to be loose and free. As you strum, you want that hand to be able to make a gesture as if you are wringing water off your hands. If you aren't able to make a smooth and swift motion then you need to reassess.

Special Note: For left handed players each of these techniques still apply except reverse each hand. Let your left hand do the strumming while your right hand frets the chords. To use this book as a left handed person simply reverse any notations of left hand with right (fret hand) and right with left (strumming hand).

Tuning

Tuning is a mystery and you'll never learn it. Let's move on.

Clearly I'm joking! Tuning your guitar is extremely important. In fact, it's the first thing you need to do every time you play and then at several varying intervals while you are performing.

I'm going to speak about standard guitar tuning. It should be noted that there are endless ways to alternatively tune your guitar, but I would recommend first learning standard tuning and then experiment with alternate tuning later.

Before we can learn about tuning, we have to know what notes each string should be tuned to. Each string, when plucked by itself, with no frets pushed down, will sound a note. In standard tuning, from lowest string [6] (which is the thickest string) to highest [1] (thinest) is: E, A, D, G, B, e. We use the big "E" for the lowest string and then the little "e" for the highest. You may not always see it written like that. Some teachers or websites reverse it but you will see it this way in most cases, including in this book.

We use numbers for our strings to help quickly identify each one. The lowest string is also the lowest sounding string. The low "E" string is considered the sixth [6] string. You count up from there. The fifth [5] string is the "A", the fourth [4] the "D", the third [3] the "G", the second [2] the "B" and the first [1] (or highest) is the "e". Again, you may see other manuals that count the highest string "e" as the sixth string and work backwards.

Now back to tuning. There are three main ways you can learn to tune: by referencing an electronic tuner, by comparing note-for-note with another instrument like a piano, or tuning by ear.

Using a digital tuning device is by far the easiest. You may want to buy an outboard tuner that you can set on your lap or the table in front of you. There are smartphone apps available that do this as well. As you play your open guitar string the pitch is analyzed by the device in front of you and you tune up or down based on the information fed back to you. If you are slightly flat then you tune upwards until you hit the exact middle of the note you are trying to tune to. If sharp, tune downwards. Be careful when tuning for the first few times not to accidentally over tune your strings beyond the note you are attempting to find. Doing so may cause the string to snap. If that happens you may be frightened to tune at all for a while. I understand that fear firsthand.

There are also tuners that clip on to the headstock of your guitar. They work via the vibrations of the guitar, which is great when onstage or in loud environments. They work the same as the tabletop tuner, however they collect their tuning data via vibration, not by hearing an audible sound. This means that if the drummer beside you is tuning his floor tom you can still be tuning your guitar. Priceless!

You may want to tune by comparing each pitch to another instrument, and if you have the ear for it, you should give it a try. This skill is worthwhile for tuning and also for learning how to hear when a pitch is flat or sharp. To tune like this you'll need to hit a reference note on the other instrument, like on a piano, that you know is in tune and then tune your string up or down until you feel like the two notes are the same. You repeat this for each note of the opened string guitar until you have completed all six strings.

Left Hand Finger Numbers

While you could use nicknames for each finger on your left hand (like pointer finger, pinky, etc.) most guitar teachers will use numbers for each finger. Using numbers allows for quick reference as you get into chord diagrams and transitioning.

Here is how I detail each finger of the left hand (again, left handed guitarists will use the reverse hand, making this diagram opposite and for the right hand). The pointer finger (index finger) is (1). Your middle finger is (2), ring finger is (3) and pinky finger (4). I label the thumb (T). While you won't get into any thumb playing in this book, you can as you improve in your skills moving on to intermediate playing.

Chords

A chord is the combination of any three or more notes played at the same time. Chords are the lifeblood of rhythm guitar playing and are one of the signature sounds that a guitar makes.

Understanding Major Versus Minor

Before you learn your first chord, it is important we settle one thing: major versus minor chords. You may be more familiar with the concept than you would think. I used to tell my younger guitar students that major chords sound happy and minor chords sound sad. It's kind of true. In practice though, you need both types of chords. You can't just be happy or sad all the time.

Major chords employ a triad (1-3-5) of the scale that makes its chord. If you were on a piano you would hear the major triad's happy tone. Minor chording changes one note: the third note of the scale is flattened (1- ♭3-5). This changes the tone of the chord completely making it sound sad. As we move forward and you learn future chords, you'll hear this distinction.

SPECIAL NOTE: While learning your chords, please don't skip ahead. Most chords (and their fingerings) build upon the knowledge of the previous chord. If you skip around you may miss some integral information.

Your First Chord!

SIMPLE "G" CHORD

Simple "G" Chord Information:
• See Chord Diagram
• Number of Strings Used: Three (3)
• Level of Difficulty: Easy
• Reminder: Practice by fretting your chord. Then take your hands off the guitar completely and try again. Repeat this process several times as you practice. Remember that transitioning to and from a chord quickly is just as important as playing the chord itself.

Perhaps the most popular chord on the planet "G" is the chord you should focus on first. You will use all four fingers of your fretting hand (left hand) by the time you master the most difficult version of this chord. But first, I recommend starting with a version that only involves one finger.

SIMPLE "G" CHORD FINGERING POSITION IN ORDER

Begin by placing your pointer finger (1) on the third fret of the high [e] string. When strumming the top three strings [G B e] you'll have forged your first chord. Practice strumming these three strings while omitting the bottom three. This is a basic "G" chord. Congratulations, you are officially a guitar player now!

INTERMEDIATE "G" CHORD

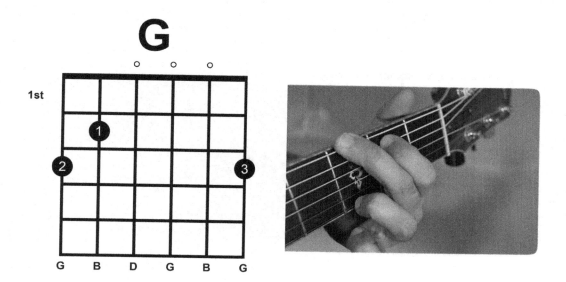

Intermediate "G" Chord Information:
• See Chord Diagram
• Number of Strings Used: Six (6)
• Level of Difficulty: Moderate
• Reminder: Practice by fretting your chord. Then take your hands off the guitar completely and try again. Repeat this process several times as you practice. Remember that transitioning to and from a chord quickly is just as important as playing the chord itself.

INTERMEDIATE "G" CHORD FINGERING POSITION IN ORDER

As you move forward, let's fret the "G" chord but use all the strings. We are going to build on the first "G" we've learned, but change our initial fingering and add two more fingers. First, place your middle finger (2) on the third fret of the low [E] string. Then squeeze your index finger (1) (which you initially used on the high [e] string) to be right next to the (2) finger, but on the [A] string on the second fret. Finally, bring your ring finger forward and place it on the third fret of the high [e] string. You'll be able to strum all six strings now and play a more full "G" chord.

FULL "G" CHORD

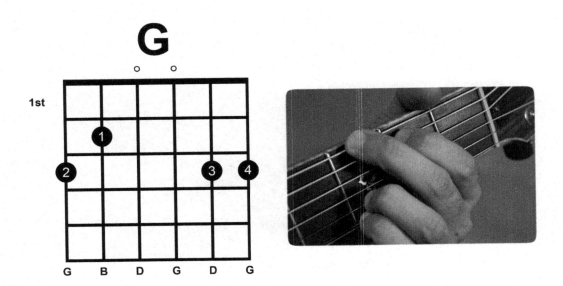

Full "G" Chord Information:
• See Chord Diagram
• Number of Strings Used: Six (6)
• Level of Difficulty: Moderate
• Reminder: Practice by fretting your chord. Then take your hands off the guitar completely and try again. Repeat this process several times as you practice. Remember that transitioning to and from a chord quickly is just as important as playing the chord itself.

FULL "G" CHORD FINGERING POSITION IN ORDER

Now for the final variation of the "G" that leaves you with the chord that you will use the most when needing to play "G". Use the fingering from the version of "G" that we just built, but move your ring finger (3) from the third fret of the [e] string to the third fret of the [B] string. Then you'll need to add your pinky finger (4) to the third fret of the [e] string. Now you have the full package "G" chord. Strum all six strings!

I make all my students show me each variation of this chord at our first lesson when we begin learning chords. You need to do the same. Practice going through each variation of this chord while taking your hand off the neck of the guitar completely between each chord change. This forces you to have to bring your hands back onto the correct frets again and again. You need to practice putting your fingers in the right place just as much as you need to practice strumming the full chord once it's in place.

For the first week plan to take your hands on and off each of these "G" positions one hundred times. As you get better at finger positioning you'll be able to do this exercise faster and faster. The practice you put in to the first few weeks of guitar will set the stage for a lifelong ability to play this instrument. You'll be building a strong foundation.

One word of caution; your hands (your left hand primarily) will probably become sore during the first month of learning. PUSH THROUGH! These are battle scars... You will be happy you stuck with this! Plus, the soreness diminishes in time.

Below is a rhythm example you can play using any of the three variations of the "G" chord. As this course develops these examples will become more intricate. You'll practice switching between chords. These are only examples. Be as creative as you'd like to be. Each slash mark indicates a down strum. There are four down strums per measure then one final strum (whole note) to end out the musical phrase. Practice!

"G" Chord Rhythm Example

- - - - -

WEEK TWO (2)

Daily Prayer For WEEK TWO

"Heavenly Father, thank you for another day that you have made. Please go before me as I learn more about the guitar. I pray that I would not only understand what I am learning but be able to teach others some day. May my memorization skills be ever expanded through your power. I pray that I would understand the concept of good rhythm and begin to build on my new skills. Please help me to be able to fret each new chord and make efficient transitions. In Jesus' name, amen."

WHAT TO EXPECT WEEK TWO

At the end of week two you should know how important practicing is to mastering guitar. You'll learn about strumming and the importance of chord transitions. You'll also have mastered the "D" and "Em" chords.

Understanding Chords

As we've said before, chords are the lifeblood of the beginning guitarist. They are what you're used to hearing on some of your favorite albums. They are usually the first thing to learn on guitar. Remember, a chord is any series of any three or more notes played simultaneously. Guitar chords are made up of as little as two notes (these are called 5ths), but can be as many as six notes (or all six strings). Most chords are actually only three notes, but have duplicating notes on higher pitches. For instance, the "G Chord" you learned is made up of these notes: G, B, D, G, D, G.

Muscle Memory

One Sunday afternoon while I was dozing in and out of sleep during a nap I awoke just enough to hear a golfer on television speak about how it takes 21 days to change his golf grip. Even if he just wants to make a slight adjustment, due to muscle memory and the way our brains achieve it, we have to do things repeatedly before mastery. There's no way to cheat or shorten that time either.

As you learn your chords, positions for your right hand or any other movement for guitar you'll need to commit to practice. Do your best to not get frustrated if you fail the first day. Think longer term. If you can't accomplish a movement after 21 days then you can be frustrated and pick up harmonica or some other instrument. Practice makes perfect and is essential.

Strumming

Strumming is the act of running your fingers (or pick/object) across multiple strings simultaneously. That can be across two or all six strings. Strumming, as opposed to picking, as we'll see in the next heading, is a practice you want to do well. Being a consistent strummer is far better than being an inconsistent one. In fact, it takes a lot of practice to keep your elbow in correct position while moving the arm in a steady motion.

First, work on the *down strum* by starting the pick (or hand if you are not using a pick) on the sixth string [E] and run it all the way through first string [e]. Practice by playing four strums as consistently as possible. Next you could practice starting with the fifth string [A], making every effort to not play the sixth [E]. Precision is key to being a great strummer.

After you've mastered the down strum, practice the *up strum*. It's like the down strum, but reversed, beginning with the first string [e] and strumming upwards to the sixth string [E]. The up strum is harder to perform consistently. It takes even more practice. Once you've mastered six strings, try omitting the sixth string [E] string, only strumming up five strings.

A special note about strumming: decades ago a friend told me a secret that changed my strumming life forever. It made my efforts to become a professional rhythm player realize faster. The secret: when playing rhythm guitar, always play down strums. Use up strums sparingly and only as accents. The down strum is king. When you count out a measure count like this: "1-e-and-a, 2-e-and-a, 3-e-and-a, 4-e-and-a". Play on beats "1" & "3" (like a kick drum in a band). Sometimes you could play down strums on beats "1", "2", "3" and "4", and leave up strums for the "and's", "e's" and "a's". As you use down strums correctly you'll notice a more defined and professional rhythm.

"D" CHORD

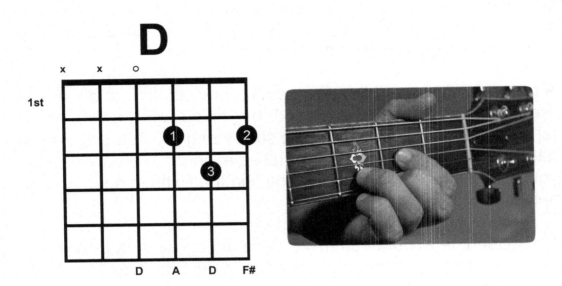

"D" Chord Information:
- See Chord Diagram
- Number of Strings Used: Four (4)
- Level of Difficulty: Easy
- Reminder: Practice by fretting your chord. Then take your hands off the guitar completely and try again. Repeat this process several times as you practice. Remember that transitioning to and from a chord quickly is just as important as playing the chord itself.

The "D" chord is about as important to learn as the "G" chord was. It is used often when playing a song that has a "G" in it, so you're ready to learn a powerful chord.

"D" CHORD FINGERING POSITION IN ORDER

Begin by placing your pointer finger (1) on the second fret of the third string [G]. Add your middle finger (2) on the second fret of the first string [e]. Lastly, add your ring finger (3) to the third fret of the second string [B]. Strum the last four strings and you are playing "D". Make sure to omit the low [E] and [A] strings when you strum this chord.

As you look at your hand that is now making the "D" chord, examine how tightly your fingers are fitting together. The secret to quick chord transition is forming each chord like a tightly packaged unit that you can get to quickly. If your hand is seemingly loose or one of your fingers is pulling away from the others, your goal should be to restrict this movement and tighten everything inward. Also, the lower you can get your fingers to the neck of the guitar the easier it will be down the road when transitioning chords. A good check for this is to fret your "D" chord and then try to put your right hand index finger into any of the holes you are making on your left hand. If you are able to poke your finger through then you need to tighten up your grip.

"D" is quite a bit easier than "G", in terms of muscle memory, because all your fingers are so close together they feel like one unit. Use our trick from the last chord exercises: put your hands on the guitar with the "D" shape and then take it off and put it back on. Do this 100 times/day over the next week and you'll build your "D" transition quickly and effectively.

Chord Transitions

Now that you have two chords learned it's very important (almost as important as learning the chords themselves) to learn how to transition your fingers into and out of each of these chords. There are two secrets to making chord transitions:

• Do not move any fingers that don't need to move. For example, transitioning from our "G" chord to our "D" chord, the ring finger (3) doesn't need to move from the 3rd fret of the 2nd [B] string. It's staying there for the "D" chord. Do your best not to let that finger come off the fretboard. Instead, use

that finger's placement as a foundational pivot point as the rest of your fingers move into place.
- Make your transition all at once. Don't let any fingers fall behind. The best practice is to try and make the transition in one motion. This increases chord transition speed and accuracy. This also makes sure that one finger isn't always trailing behind, which is a "no-no!".

Use the rhythm example below to develop your transitioning skills while practicing your new "D" chord.

"D" Chord Rhythm Example

"Em" CHORD

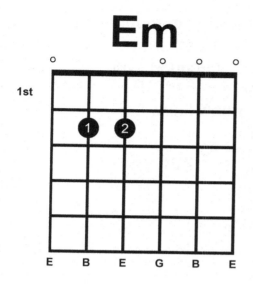

"Em" Chord Information:
• See Chord Diagram
• Number of Strings Used: Six (6)
• Level of Difficulty: Easy
• Reminder: Practice by fretting your chord. Then take your hands off the guitar completely and try again. Repeat this process several times as you practice. Remember that transitioning to and from a chord quickly is just as important as playing the chord itself.

"Em" CHORD FINGERING POSITION IN ORDER

Place your pointer finger (1) onto the second fret of the 5th string [A]. Please notice that this finger is on the same fret/string as it is in your "G" chord, which will prove useful as you make transitions between these chords. Next, and finally, as this chord is easy to fret, add your middle finger (2) to the second fret of the 4th string [D]. The Em chord only uses two fingers from the left hand and then a full strum of all six strings.

This is the first minor chord you've learned. Begin to practice going from the major chord "G" into the minor chord "Em". Go back and forth as fast as you can while keeping perfect positioning with your fingers. Do not allow for imperfection. That means: go slow at first and only add speed as you master the transition. You'll be glad you did because you will have reinforced good habits and not added any bad. Use the following rhythm examples using all chords you now know.

"Em" Chord Rhythm Example

"Em" Chord Rhythm Example

- - - - -

WEEK THREE (3)

Daily Prayer For WEEK THREE

"Heavenly Father, thank you for this day and that I've learned so much in the last few weeks. Please help me to understand these new concepts. May my fingers fall into perfect position as I learn new chords. May they build on the foundation of the ones that have gone before. I pray that this week would be a breakthrough week in my pursuit of music. I welcome you to help me as I go. In Jesus' name, amen."

WHAT TO EXPECT WEEK THREE

By the end of week three you should be able to pick out the perfect guitar strap and guitar picks for you. You'll understand the difference between picking and finger picking. And you'll know the "C" and "Am" chords.

Guitar Straps

If you'd like to stand and perform at any point you'll need a guitar strap. Guitar straps are often made of leather or polyester and are long strips of material that connect to the upper and lower body of your guitar. They are there to hold the guitar in place using your shoulder as support while you stand. Straps come in various designs and materials. There is no right or wrong in your choice. It's all about your preference. I've seen people use shoe strings as straps. The main thing is that the strap is secure and holds the guitar. You don't want your guitar to fall to the ground and break.

If your guitar does not have two strap pegs already installed on your guitar you may consider having them installed by a guitar technician at your local music shop. I would not attempt to add them yourself because this involves drilling into your guitar. If it only has one peg at the bottom you can either install a second one at the top of the body or you can use a string to connect it at the bottom of the headstock. Either position works.

Guitar Picks

Guitar picks are usually small, thin pieces of hard plastic designed to fit in your right thumb and pointer finger and used to strike the strings. Picks come in tons of different shapes, sizes and textures. I recommend purchasing a bag of *light*, plastic picks. As you progress on the guitar you can try out different kinds of picks. Harder picks will make the guitar sound louder and brighter. Softer picks will make it softer and milder. You should experiment.

Picking

Picking, unlike strumming, aims at playing individual strings, rather than multiple at once. While some notes will carry over while picking, it's a unique sound. To begin, you'll need to purchase a *pick* at your local guitar or online music store. Begin by plucking one string at a time. You can then alternate strings or even do high then low then middle. As you learn future chords, picking will come in handy.

Finger Picking

Finger picking is the most difficult way to play consistently on a guitar. While I won't go into detail on how to do it (although YouTube would) I will say that it is how it sounds. You make your hand into a claw-like shape and then, as though each of your fingers are picks, you pluck strings individually with your fingers. It's hard to stay consistent while finger picking as a beginning guitar player. Most of your attention has to be placed at keeping an eye of your left hand and the chords you are making. While finger picking, your right hand also needs attention.

"C" CHORD

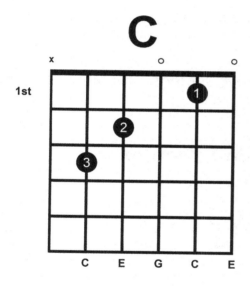

"C" Chord Information:
• See Chord Diagram
• Number of Strings Used: Five (5)
• Level of Difficulty: Moderate
• Reminder: Practice by fretting your chord. Then take your hands off the guitar completely and try again. Repeat this process several times as you practice. Remember that

transitioning to and from a chord quickly is just as important as playing the chord itself.

"C" CHORD FINGERING POSITION IN ORDER

The "C" chord may prove the most difficult of the chords we've learned so far. Push through this one and then some of the following chords we learn will be smoother sailing.

Begin by placing the index finger (1) on the first fret of the 2nd string [B]. Make sure you make excellent contact with that string without muting the 3rd [G] and 1st [e] strings around it. You can strum those top three strings to confirm your position. Next, add your middle finger (2) to the second fret of the 4th string [D], again making great contact. Finally add your ringer finger (3) to the third fret of the 5th string [A]. Realizing that this will feel like a tough stretch, make sure you have have excellent posture as you place your hands on the guitar. Do not let your left hand slouch. Strum this chord using the last five strings, muting or not strumming the sixth string [E].

"C" Chord Rhythm Example

"Am" CHORD

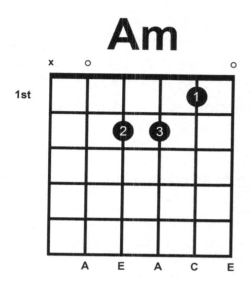

"Am" Chord Information:
• See Chord Diagram
• Number of Strings Used: Five (5)
• Level of Difficulty: Moderate
• Reminder: Practice by fretting your chord. Then take your hands off the guitar completely and try again. Repeat this process several times as you practice. Remember that transitioning to and from a chord quickly is just as important as playing the chord itself.

"Am" CHORD FINGERING POSITION IN ORDER

After learning the "C" chord, the "Am" is it's perfect cousin. Begin by fretting the "C" chord you just learned. To make the "Am" you only need to move your ring finger (3) from the 3rd fret of the 5th string [A] to the second fret of the 3rd string [G]. If you'll keep great hand posture and strum the last five strings, just like the "C" chord, you'll have the "Am".

Were you to have to build the chord from scratch without coming from the "C" chord, it would form this way. Place the index finger (1) on the first fret of the 2nd string [B]. Then, add your middle finger (2) to the second fret of the 4th string [D]. Finally add your ringer finger (3) to the second fret of the 3rd string [G]. You may be noticing the tight squeeze of all three fingers so close together. This is normal. With good up and down pressure and zero left to right slouching all three fingers will fit in their proper place.

"Am" Chord Rhythm Example

- - - - -

WEEK FOUR (4)

Daily Prayer For WEEK FOUR

"Heavenly Father, I thank you again for a new day to honor You. I praise you that I'm over halfway through this guitar training. Please help me to play in time and in tune. Help me to learn these new concepts. I pray that I would build on the foundation from weeks past and that these new chords would be quick to attain. May my fingers callous well and not hurt. Thank you God! In Jesus' name, amen."

WHAT TO EXPECT WEEK FOUR

By the end of week four you will know how to use a metronome and a capo. You'll also learn the "A", "E" and "Bm" chords.

Metronome

The mighty metronome takes no prisoners! A metronome is both loved and hated by professional musicians. A metronome is a device that keeps perfect time. The metronome creates click sounds that are on beats 1, 2, 3, and 4. The musician or band attempts to stay in perfect time with it. It's very important as you learn to play guitar that you consistently play with a metronome.

It will help you to play in time. The better you are with a metronome the better you will play without one. Some of the best musicians in the world play in perfect time. I believe that it separates the pros from those who aren't professional. You can get a physical metronome from your local music store or online. Also, if you have a smart phone you can download an app and always have your *met* with you in your pocket!

Understanding The Capo

The capo is among the mightiest of tools. A capo is a tool used to raise the pitch of all the strings it lays across. For instance, playing a "G" chord without a capo will give you a "G" chord. If you put a capo across the entire 2nd fret and play that same "G" chord shape, you now have moved everything up two frets and you're playing an "A" chord, but using the "G" fingering. This is useful for two reasons. Sometimes playing the "G" chord shape is easier. The other reason is because the top note being played is the tonic note (or the root note) instead of the fifth note in the scale, like when using an "A" shape. You can hear the difference. There are times when having the root note on top will make the most sense, especially if the melody being sung is singing the root as well. I'm sorry to have gone into a bit of music theory. My point being, the capo is a great tool!

Please don't let anyone ever tell you that using a capo is like a bicycle that has training wheels. Those people never had the proper understanding of how powerful a tool it can be. Some of the greatest guitar players use capos as part of their signature sound. The Beatles' song "Here Comes The Sun" is played with a capo on the seventh fret. When Chris Tomlin plays "How Great Is Our God", he plays it in "G" but capoed on the fifth fret.

"A" CHORD

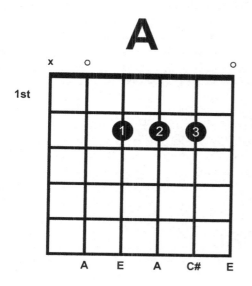

"A" Chord Information:
• See Chord Diagram
• Number of Strings Used: Five (5)
• Level of Difficulty: Moderate
• Reminder: Practice by fretting your chord. Then take your hands off the guitar completely and try again. Repeat this process several times as you practice. Remember that transitioning to and from a chord quickly is just as important as playing the chord itself.

"A" CHORD FINGERING POSITION IN ORDER

There are multiple fingerings for the standard "A" chord. I'm going to demonstrate the main version; however, future books or the internet may show you others. Begin by placing your index finger (1) onto the 2nd fret of the 4th string [D]. Continue by placing your middle finger (2) onto the 2nd fret of the 3rd string [G]. Last, place your ring finger (3) on the 2nd fret of the 2nd string [B]. Strum the last five strings, omitting the low [E] string.

You need to practice getting into this position over and over before muscle memory will develop. This is a tough beginner chord, so don't despair if this one takes more time than preceding chords.

"A" Chord Rhythm Example

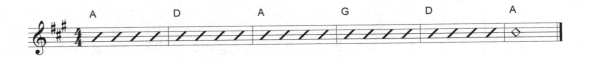

"E" CHORD

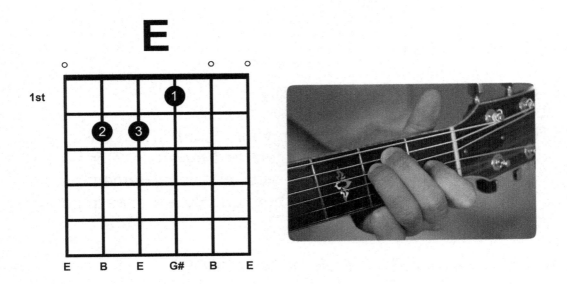

"E" Chord Information:
- See Chord Diagram
- Number of Strings Used: Six (6)
- Level of Difficulty: Moderate
- Reminder: Practice by fretting your chord. Then take your hands off the guitar completely and try again. Repeat this

process several times as you practice. Remember that transitioning to and from a chord quickly is just as important as playing the chord itself.

"E" CHORD FINGERING POSITION IN ORDER

Many, many worship songs and hymns utilize the "E" chord. Start by placing your middle finger (2) on the 2nd fret of the 5th string [A]. Then set your ring finger (3) onto the 2nd fret of the 4th string [D]. Finally, and this takes some stretching, place your index finger (1) on the 1st fret of the 3rd string [G]. Strum all six strings. The tendency to let up on the 3rd string is enticing at first. Doing so changes the tone of the chord. Be intentional in keeping strong contact with the fretboard and strings.

"E" Chord Rhythm Example

Barre Chords

You are now ready for your first barre chord. A barre chord is a way of fingering a chord by holding down the same fret number over several strings using only one finger. Barre chords are tough, but achievable.

"Bm" CHORD

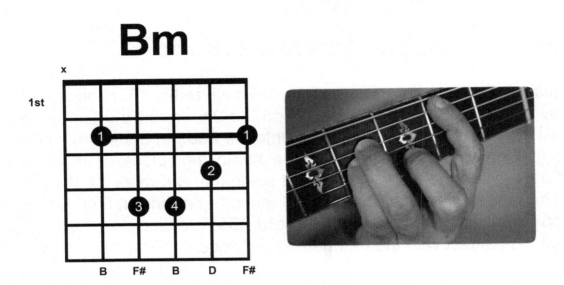

Bm

"Bm" Chord Information:
* See Chord Diagram
* Number of Strings Used: Five (5)
* Level of Difficulty: Difficult
* Reminder: Practice by fretting your chord. Then take your hands off the guitar completely and try again. Repeat this process several times as you practice. Remember that transitioning to and from a chord quickly is just as important as playing the chord itself.

"Bm" CHORD FINGERING POSITION IN ORDER

Our first barre chord is "Bm". Begin by taking your index finger (1) and lay it at as flat as you can across the 2nd fret of all five strings beginning at the 5th string [A] on to the 1st string [e]. You can omit the 6th string [E] for this chord, which is a minor blessing in disguise, as the thicker the string, the tougher it is to barre. After you feel that you're keeping a strong grip across all five strings, begin placing the other fingers onto the fretboard.

The first additional finger to add is your middle finger (2) onto the 3rd fret of the 2nd string [B]. Confirm that your barre has not lost it's strength. Last, add your ring finger (3) and your pinky finger (4) to the 4th frets of the 4th [D] and 3rd [G] strings, respectively. Once all fingers are in place you will strum the last five strings, leaving out the 6th sting [E] that isn't being pressed down. Do not despair if you've lost some of your grip and the sound is puny or nonexistent. This is a very hard chord! Take your hand off the guitar and begin the sequence of fretting again. Over time you will develop the dexterity to achieve this and many of the other barre chords.

"Bm" Chord Rhythm Example

- - - - -

WEEK FIVE (5)

Daily Prayer For WEEK FIVE

"Heavenly Father, thank you for this good day. Please go before me as I am learning so much more about guitar. I pray that the skill that I am developing would forever be a strong musical foundation for all that I do. As I begin to play with other musicians, please help me to be wise in my pursuits. May I always look for your character in them as I make connections. Today, please help my fingers to fall in correct places and make quick and strong transitions as I chord. In Jesus' name, amen."

WHAT TO EXPECT WEEK FIVE

By the end of week five you'll know how to select and change your guitar strings. You'll also have learned the tough "F" and "Dm" chords.

Choosing The Right Strings

Guitar strings are the lifeblood of a guitar. They are normally made of hard metal and come in various thicknesses. You'll notice that they are around 3-4 feet long and have a small ball on the end of each string. You can purchase them with or without coating. Coating is a protective layer of material laid over the metal on the string and is said to increase string life. As you touch your strings your fingers leave acid residue which builds up over time. That residue causes the strings to become dull. You can actually feel the string itself and tell that it has built up too much residue. That means it's time to change strings. Depending on how often you play, that could mean you need to change your strings as often as each month or as little as every six months. I recommend not letting your strings go longer than six months.

I recommend purchasing a set of *light* strings. That means that the thickness of each string will be in what is considered the guitar string *light* class. Typically that means your highest string 1 [e] will have a gauge of .10 - .12 mm. *Light* strings are easier to push down on the fretboard than medium strings, but not as easy as super light strings. For beginners, in my opinion, they are just the right size.

While there may seem to be about 100 brands and styles, simply choose a package or two of strings that meet your budget. A normal package of professional, non-coated acoustic guitar strings should cost around $6. Coated strings, which may last longer, should cost $10-$13. I use coated strings because I play so often. For your first sets of strings, you may consider buying regular strings and then upgrading as you get better; especially as you play more often.

How To Change Strings

Changing your own guitar strings is a skill you should acquire. Yes, the store where you buy your strings will put them on for you, but they usually charge for that. Plus, when you change your own strings you get to confirm that there aren't any new chips in the body. You identify any problems that have arisen. Also, you get to clean your guitar. The shop isn't gong to take near as much care for your instrument as you will.

To replace old strings with new ones, I typically follow this method and order. You can attempt other methods, but this is what I and some other professionals do.

First, remove the old strings. Do this by loosening the tuning pegs to the point where the string you want released can be pulled out of its hole. I like to loosen all six strings from the headstock before removing them from the body. Once all strings are off, throw them away. They are old, used and not worth keeping. Not even as spares. Most music stores sell individual new strings, if you feel like you want to have some as spares. Old strings are stretched out and often covered in finger residue. They are spent.

Next, I clean the guitar and neck. I use guitar cleaner or polish for the body, back of neck and headstock, but not the front of the neck. Make sure you get all finger prints and any unwanted residue off your guitar. For the neck, I use a guitar-specific lemon oil. It refreshes the wood of the neck while still cleaning your frets. Lastly, and this is only for instruments with a sound hole (like an acoustic guitar), I take compressed spray air (often used to clean electronics) and spray out any dust in the chamber of the body. When dust settles inside the body it causes sound to vibrate in a different way than the guitar was designed to thus changing or dampening its tone.

After you've sufficiently cleaned your guitar you can move on to putting on your new strings. I recommend beginning with the thickest string [E6]. Most acoustic guitars have a tooth-like pin that needs to be pushed back in after you've inserted the ball bottom of the new string. Once in place you should be able to stretch the string the entire length of the guitar and neck. Put the end of the string into the first hole on the left side of the tuner area on the headstock. I recommend making sure that as you begin turning the tuning peg the string be wound so that it moves the end of the string move toward the middle of the headstock. This is rather than having the string wind toward the outside of the guitar. In other words, for the sixth, fifth and fourth string, the strings should wind counterclockwise and the third, second, and first should wind clockwise. If all tuning pegs are on one side I still recommend winding to the center of the neck.

A secret that I learned a long time ago about how to wind your strings so that they tightly hold and stay in tune is to let the end of the wound string first go UNDER the string being tuned. After the string has been under once, make the remaining turns go OVER the string being tuned. It creates a type of locking mechanism.

Repeat the steps above for all remaining strings. You should now have all new strings on your guitar. Congratulations!

You'll need to do a few final steps before you are ready to tune up. First, you'll need to stretch out your new strings. This gets any leftover loose slack out at the strings at the headstock. It also lets the strings themselves begin to balance. They came from the factory pretty rigid. To stretch your strings, begin by pulling them off the guitar neck about 2-3 inches. Be safe! You want to stretch them at three second intervals for three to fives sets, releasing the string in between. After you have sufficiently stretched your strings it will be time to cut the ends of the strings that are still hanging on at the headstock. Be careful when using wire cutters or sharp scissors. Also, make sure you are cutting off the string excess and not the actual string that is new and on the guitar. I have made that mistake before and it's not fun. Finally, use needle nose pliers to bend the tiny ends of the strings down and into the headstock. Your goal should be to not have any dangerous metal sticking out toward you to make you bleed if you were to touch that area. I always keep a bandaid in my guitar string changing kit. Ha!

"F" CHORD

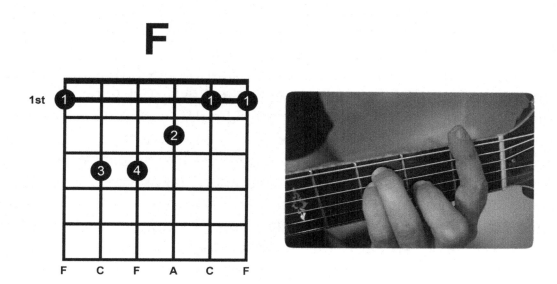

F

1st

F   C   F   A   C   F

"F" Chord Information:
• See Chord Diagram
• Number of Strings Used: Six (6)
• Level of Difficulty: Difficult
• Reminder: Practice by fretting your chord. Then take your hands off the guitar completely and try again. Repeat this process several times as you practice. Remember that transitioning to and from a chord quickly is just as important as playing the chord itself.

"F" CHORD FINGERING POSITION IN ORDER

For most beginning guitarists, the "F" chord is considered the hardest of the barre chords to learn. It looks similar to the "Bm" that you've already learned, but it uses all six strings, barres three strings (instead of 2 like the Bm) and sits on the first fret, which is closest to the nut. Even though it is rough at first, you most certainly can master the chord.

The first step is to lay your index finger (1) across all six strings on the first fret. You need to press down all the strings so that you get clarity out of each note. Take your time in trying to get tonal clarity before moving forward. It will help to lay a strong foundation for the "F" chord. Now that you have the 1st finger in place add your ring (3) and pinky (4) finger on the 3rd frets of the 5th [A] and 4th [D] strings respectively. Last, add your middle finger (2) onto the 2nd fret of the 3rd [G] string. Once all in place, you should be able to strum across all six strings and produce an "F" chord. The first few times you may have fret buzz or may not be able to produce sound at all. This chord takes more practice than any we've introduced before. To rehearse this, take your hand off the guitar and then position the "F" chord. Practice this over and over. Eventually you'll have a strong "F".

"F" Chord Rhythm Example

"Dm" CHORD

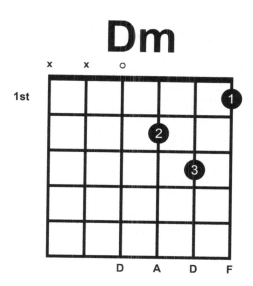

"Dm" Chord Information:
- See Chord Diagram
- Number of Strings Used: Four (4)
- Level of Difficulty: Easy
- Reminder: Practice by fretting your chord. Then take your hands off the guitar completely and try again. Repeat this process several times as you practice. Remember that transitioning to and from a chord quickly is just as important as playing the chord itself.

"Dm" CHORD FINGERING POSITION IN ORDER

"Dm" is a close relative to the "F" chord, but is much, much easier to play! Begin by placing your middle finger (2) on the 2nd fret of the third [G] string. Add the ring finger (3) to the 3rd fret of the 2nd [B] string. Finally, put your index finger (1) on the 1st fret of the 1st [e] string. Once in place, strum the last four strings.

"Dm" Chord Rhythm Example

- - - - -

WEEK SIX (6)

Daily Prayer For WEEK SIX

"Heavenly Father, thank you for this great day! I praise you that I made it to the last week of *Worship Guitar In Six Weeks*. May I remember all that I've learned. May you richly bless this final week. I pray that I would understand some of the deeper philosophies of music notation. That my hands would fall into the right places for some of the tougher chords that I am learning. Thank you for how you've helped me throughout this experience. In Jesus' name, amen."

WHAT TO EXPECT WEEK SIX

By the end of week six you'll know the difference between many types of sheet music. You will also have mastered three difficult chords: "B", "C#m" and "F#m".

Chord Charts

It's important that as a musician (not just a guitar player, but a musician) that you learn how to read sheet music. The most basic way you'll see music is the "chords over words" method, or chord charts. This is when you'll see a chord written directly over top of the lyric being sung. You only make a chord transition when the words change. This is the easiest form of "sheet music" to create because it only takes a word processor, like Microsoft Word™ to create. Unfortunately though, this is the least accurate form of sheet music. The placement of the chords can sometimes seem arbitrary. Also, what about the times when the singer isn't singing, like in an intro or turnaround? Due to its simple nature, you'll may see these type of charts. They aren't bad, they're just insufficient.

Guitar Tablature (Tabs)

Searching the Internet you'll find lots and lots of *guitar tabs* (or guitar tablature). Similar in nature to chords over words charts, guitar tabs are easily made in word processors. They look a bit like sheet music, but the lines going across your page or screen represent strings. Therefore you'll see six lines. On those lines you'll see numbers. Each number represents a fret being pressed down. For example (320033) is the "G" chord you've learned. What this doesn't tell you is when to play the "G" or, in the case of a chord you don't know, which finger to put on the assigned frets. Guitar tabs are really helpful once you've gotten your feet wet with guitar and want to learn a specific part that someone has transcribed. As an aside, I will warn you that most guitar tabs available online are highly inaccurate. I've seen some really wrong ways to play famous songs, while the tab claims to be 100% accurate.

Sheet Music (Staff Music)

Sheet music, or staff music is the oldest form of written music and has the highest accuracy of any transcription available. Beethoven used sheet music. Bono uses sheet music. Sheet music can be complicated, like a Bach piece, or it can be simple. Most worship music that you'll purchase is a simple form of sheet music, called a *lead sheet*. You'll see rhythm notes, chords and standard notes with the lyrics written below them. There are measure indications so you'll know where a measure starts and ends. There are also indications such as dynamic cues (louder/softer) and tempo cues (ritard). Sheet music is typically created by professionals, thus it costs money. There are several resources (searchable on Google) that will provide free sheet music each week. These are worth subscribing to.

Nashville Numbers System

The Nashville numbers system is the final form of sheet music I'll describe. I won't stay long on this form of sheet music, because it is primarily used by professionals. The basic premise is that the tonic chord is your "1 chord", then your respective chords get assigned a number based on where they sit in the scale. In the key of "A", for example, the 1 chord is an A, the 2m chord is a Bm, the 3m chord is a C#m and so on. The difficulty with this type of notation is that the player has to "really know his numbers" - as they say. You have to know what chords do and do not belong in the key of "A". You also have to do math in your head as the chords change, which isn't easy to do on the fly. I do recommend trying to learn this type of notation, but leave it for as you progress!

"B" CHORD

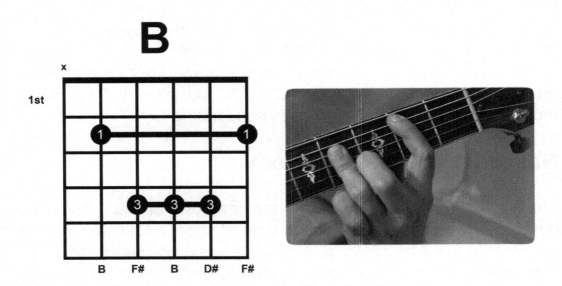

B   F#   B   D#   F#

"B" Chord Information:
• See Chord Diagram
• Number of Strings Used: Five (5)
• Level of Difficulty: Difficult
• Reminder: Practice by fretting your chord. Then take your hands off the guitar completely and try again. Repeat this process several times as you practice. Remember that transitioning to and from a chord quickly is just as important as playing the chord itself.

"B" CHORD FINGERING POSITION IN ORDER

The "B" chord is a barre chord like "F" and "Bm", but includes two barres rather than just one. Initially the "B" may feel impossible, but it can be done with time and practice. The "B" is important because it often used when playing in the key of "E".

Start fingering the "B" by setting your index finger (1) on the 2nd fret across the bottom five strings, omitting the 6th [E] string.

Before we start the second barre, it's important that you've got a strong hold on the second fret. Once in place, take your ring finger (3) and attempt to barre the 4th fret of the 4th, 3rd, and 2nd strings. It's very important that you do not cover up the 1st string that the index finger (1) is currently pressing down on the 2nd fret. You strum the last five strings, omitting the sixth string. Practice putting your fingers on and off the "B" shape. This chord has the potential to cause finger pain until you develop callouses.

"B" Chord Rhythm Example

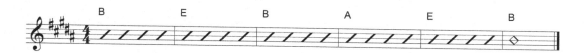

"C#m" CHORD

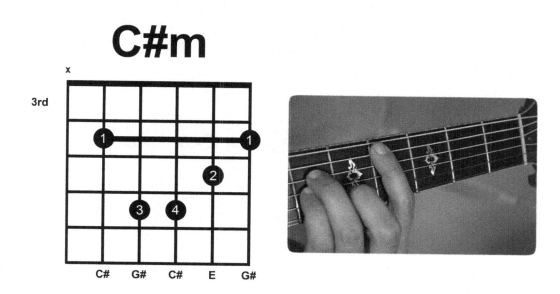

"C#m" Chord Information:
• See Chord Diagram
• Number of Strings Used: Five (5)

- Level of Difficulty: Difficult
- Reminder: Practice by fretting your chord. Then take your hands off the guitar completely and try again. Repeat this process several times as you practice. Remember that transitioning to and from a chord quickly is just as important as playing the chord itself.

"C#m" CHORD FINGERING POSITION IN ORDER

"C#m" looks exactly like "Bm" that you've learned, except that it is two frets higher on the neck of your guitar. Begin by taking your index finger (1) and lay it at as flat as you can across the 4th fret of all five strings, beginning at the 5th string [A] all the way across to the 1st string [e]. You can omit the 6th string [E] for this chord. The next finger to add is your middle finger (2) onto the 5th fret of the 2nd string [B]. Remember to be sure that your barre has not lost its strength. Lastly, add your ring finger (3) and your pinky finger (4) to the 6th frets of the 4th [D] and 3rd [G] strings respectively. Once all fingers are in place, you will only strum the last five strings, leaving out the 6th sting [E] that isn't being pressed down. Take your hand off the guitar and begin the sequence of fretting again. As with your other chords, you'll need to practice this chord often.

"C#m" Chord Rhythm Example

"F#m" CHORD

F#m

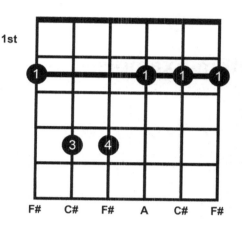

"F#m" Chord Information:
- See Chord Diagram
- Number of Strings Used: Six (6)
- Level of Difficulty: Difficult
- Reminder: Practice by fretting your chord. Then take your hands off the guitar completely and try again. Repeat this process several times as you practice. Remember that transitioning to and from a chord quickly is just as important as playing the chord itself.

"F#m" CHORD FINGERING POSITION IN ORDER

The final chord that is covered in this book is "F#m". Please note, this is NOT "Fm", but rather "F#m". The "#" matters as it is one half step higher in pitch than an "F". Also different is that this is a minor chord, not major.

The first step is to lay your index finger (1) across all six strings on the second fret. Next add your ring (3) and pinky (4) finger on the 4th frets of the 5th [A] and 4th [D] strings, respectively. Once all in place, you should be able to strum across all six strings and produce an "F#m" chord. Be careful to make sure you hear all six strings completely. It's important that you hear the 2nd fret note on the 3rd [G] string as that is what is making the chord a minor chord.

"F#m" Chord Rhythm Example

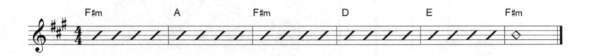

- - - - -

Final Greetings

Now that you've learned all 13 chords in *Worship Guitar In Six Weeks* it's time to start performing with others! Perhaps you could check into your church's worship team. You also may be ready to lead a small group in worship (with you singing or someone else leading). The important part is to keep playing. You will lose some of your dexterity when you don't practice. Also, playing with others, especially those who are better than you, will sharpen your skills 2:1 as compared to playing by yourself. You don't have to play with only guitar players. Any instrument you play with will challenge you in ways you haven't been challenged before.

Blessing!

"I pray that all you have begun by learning guitar as an instrument will be used mightily for the kingdom of God. That the LORD would honor your investment in His kingdom as you go forward worshiping Him. May God lead you in all you do and open wide the gates of heaven to you! In Jesus' name, amen."

Appendix

A Note About Selecting Your Guitar

"Friends never let friends go into a guitar store alone." Never go into a guitar store to buy a guitar without facts about the price and availability of that guitar in your area. Most music store salesmen are about as motivated as used car salesmen. They know which guitars have the highest margin. If you go into your store without a plan you may come out with your salesman's favorite pick, but may not be the best guitar for you in the long run. My recommendation is that you take with you an experienced guitar player whom you trust.

Also, a quick note about price range: I'm often asked "What guitar should I get?". My answer is always the same: "What's your price range?". Acoustic guitars in particular live in specific price bands. The entry level acoustic: $100-$300. The intermediate: $500-$1,000. And the professional: $1,000 and up. I intentionally left out the $300-$500 range. The biggest difference between an entry level and an intermediate guitar is the type of wood and binding that the luthier, or guitar maker, uses to create the instrument. You will find a better instrument after you cross the $500 barrier. Normally, you will not notice a significant difference between a guitar for $250 and one for $400. I recommend folks stay in the $250-$300 range. You may find an acoustic guitar for $299 and then the same guitar for $449, but with electronics (making it an acoustic electric guitar). Don't be fooled into paying that extra $150 for electronics that cost the manufacturer $8 to install. The majority of their cost is in drilling the holes in the wood. Rather, buy the nicest $299 acoustic guitar you can find and then add the electronics later. You'll be glad you did. The sound quality when plugged in will be much better. When you begin to look at intermediate or professional guitars is when I would consider an onboard pickup and electronics package that come pre-installed. Most of the time those pickups are hand selected for that particular instrument and are part of the guitar's original design.

While you are negotiating the final price for your guitar, consider asking for a few items as part of a bundle. You will want a new set of strings. You don't know how long that guitar has been on the shelf, being played by who knows how many people. You'll also need a strap (get one you like), a tuner (if you have a smart phone you could download an app), and you'll want to buy a capo. The capo is discussed in greater detail in WEEK FOUR of this book.

Finally, spring for the hardshell case that is made for your guitar. Unlike a grand piano that moves once a decade, your guitar is small enough to go places. It will be in your trunk with all your baseball gear. Maybe your little sister will have to sit on it in the middle row of your parent's minivan. Who knows? Get the case that fits the guitar snugly so that it is supremely protected when you aren't performing or practicing. Again, you'll be glad you took this advice.

To sum up, go to your music store with a plan (and with a musician friend) and be prepared to negotiate for a bundled price. Also, remember to budget for a hardshell case if you are able. Some stores may want to sell you a warranty. While I'm sure it seems tempting, typically warrantees have deductibles and aren't worth all they are said to be worth. Since you may be buying a lower end instrument (especially if this is your first), know that you are going to get scratches, bumps and bruises on it. You may want to disregard the store's warranty pitch.

Chord Families Diagram

The diagram below will help you know what chords belong in which chord families. For instance, in the key of "G", the "G" chord is the most important with the "C" and "D" chords being secondarily important. In the key of "D" the "D" is most important while the "G" and "A" are secondary. Use this diagram to become more familiar with keys and chord families.

Chord Families

Key	1	2m	1/3	4	5	6m	5/7	1
G	G	Am	G/B	C	D	Em	D/F#	G
A	A	Bm	A/C#	D	E	F#m	E/G#	A
B	B	C#m	B/D#	E	F#	G#m	F#/A#	B
C	C	Dm	C/E	F	G	Am	G/B	C
D	D	Em	D/F#	G	A	Bm	A/C#	D
E	E	F#m	E/G#	A	B	C#m	B/D#	E
F	F	Gm	F/A	Bb	C	Dm	C/E	F

About The Author

My name is Micah Brooks and I'm a worship leader from Nashville, Tennessee, USA. My passion is to see Jesus' people lift up and worship Jesus' name. I first picked up guitar at the age of thirteen. Having never taken a lesson I learned to play using training manuals, much like this one. If you calculate from the date that I write this, I have been playing guitar for over eighteen years. At age eighteen I began my first paid gigs as a musician. I suppose that was the point when I became a professional. Who knows? Since then I have used the guitar to lead worship for thousands of people. The guitar is one of the greatest tools we have for modern worship. When the guitar is used to expand God's kingdom the opportunities are endless. All glory to Jesus Christ!

Additional Resources

Find out about the other books in this series and sign up for the Micah Brooks "Stay Connected" mailing list.

This is book one in the Micah Brooks Guitar Authority Series books. This first book, *Worship Guitar In Six Weeks,* is a six week course designed to bring a guitar player from knowing little about guitar onto the stage in six weeks. The second book is *42 Guitar Chords Everyone Should Know. Guitar Secrets Revealed* is the third book and is intended to be for intermediate to experienced guitar players.

Find out about the Micah Brooks Guitar Authority Series books and more at:

www.micahbrooks.com

Email Micah

Email Micah Brooks at micah@micahbrooks.com. I want to know who you are. I have a heart to meet people. It is my privilege to respond to my emails personally. Please feel free to connect with me. I will glad to answer questions or set up a Skype call as you need.

Join the Micah Brooks "Stay Connected" mailing list

Subscribe to the Micah Brooks Ministry "Stay Connected" mailing list and stay current with my latest book releases. My email list is always free and intended to deliver high value content to your inbox. I do not sell your email address to anyone else. I simply want to be able to stay connected with you. Click here to join my mailing list.

www.micahbrooks.com/join

Reviews on Amazon

Reviews are the lifeblood of authors. If you are willing to leave feedback, I would be humbled and grateful. Please do so at:

www.amazon.com

Skype Lessons

I would be glad to consider giving you online guitar lessons. If you would like to apply for lessons with Micah Brooks via Skype visit my website to find out more. I cannot accept every student, but I would be happy to hear your story and see what you would like to accomplish. Visit micahbrooks.com.

Join The Christian Guitar Community Facebook Group

All readers of this book are welcome to join The Christian Guitar Community Facebook group. Meet guitar players from around the world. You may post your insights about learning guitar. You are welcome to ask questions and comment on other posts. The group is designed to be a community. We ask everyone in the group to interact, which makes the content fun and engaging.

www.facebook.com/groups/thechristianguitarcommunity

Visit **micahbrooks.com** for more about Micah Brooks including books, CDs, mp3s, online store, speaking and performing dates.

Made in the USA
Columbia, SC
04 April 2018